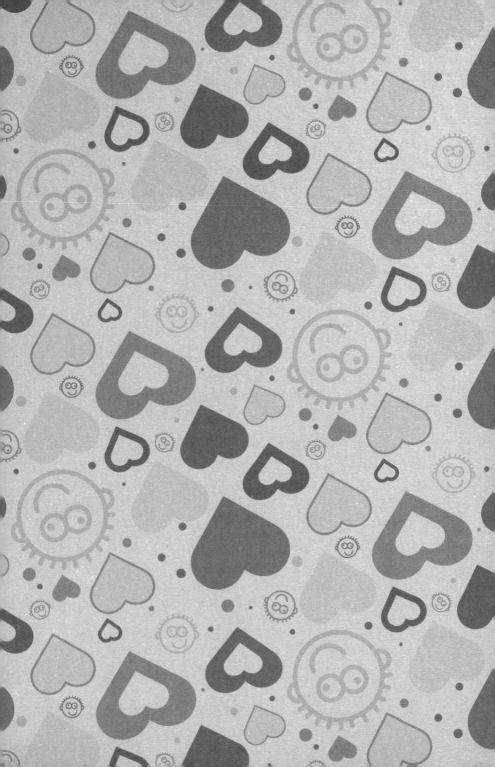

Happy Valentine's Day!

Love, MAD LIBS®

MAD LIBS
An Imprint of Penguin Random House LLC, New York

Mad Libs format and text copyright © 2009, 2019 by Penguin Random House LLC. All rights reserved.

Concept created by Roger Price & Leonard Stern

Illustration for *Valentine's Day Mad Libs* by Scott Brooks

Happy Valentine's Day! Love, Mad Libs published in 2019 by Mad Libs,
an imprint of Penguin Random House LLC, New York.
Manufactured in China.

Visit us online at www.penguinrandomhouse.com.

Happy Valentine's Day! Love, Mad Libs ISBN 9781524793395
1 3 5 7 9 10 8 6 4 2

MAD LIBS is a registered trademark of Penguin Random House LLC.

MAD LIBS

INSTRUCTIONS

MAD LIBS® is a game for people who don't like games! It can be played by one, two, three, four, or forty.

• RIDICULOUSLY SIMPLE DIRECTIONS

In this tablet you will find stories containing blank spaces where words are left out. One player, the READER, selects one of these stories. The READER does not tell anyone what the story is about. Instead, he/she asks the other players, the WRITERS, to give him/her words. These words are used to fill in the blank spaces in the story.

• TO PLAY

The READER asks each WRITER in turn to call out a word—an adjective or a noun or whatever the space calls for—and uses them to fill in the blank spaces in the story. The result is a MAD LIBS® game.

When the READER then reads the completed MAD LIBS® game to the other players, they will discover that they have written a story that is fantastic, screamingly funny, shocking, silly, crazy, or just plain dumb—depending upon which words each WRITER called out.

• EXAMPLE (*Before* and *After*)

" _____ !" he said _____
        EXCLAMATION   ADVERB

as he jumped into his convertible _____ and
                                                    NOUN

drove off with his _____ wife.
                          ADJECTIVE

" _____ **OUCH** _____ !" he said _____ **HAPPILY** _____
        EXCLAMATION   ADVERB

as he jumped into his convertible _____ **CAT** _____ and
                                                    NOUN

drove off with his _____ **BRAVE** _____ wife.
                          ADJECTIVE

In case you have forgotten what adjectives, adverbs, nouns, and verbs are, here is a quick review:

An ADJECTIVE describes something or somebody. *Lumpy, soft, ugly, messy,* and *short* are adjectives.

An ADVERB tells how something is done. It modifies a verb and usually ends in "ly." *Modestly, stupidly, greedily,* and *carefully* are adverbs.

A NOUN is the name of a person, place, or thing. *Sidewalk, umbrella, bridle, bathtub,* and *nose* are nouns.

A VERB is an action word. *Run, pitch, jump,* and *swim* are verbs. Put the verbs in past tense if the directions say PAST TENSE. *Ran, pitched, jumped,* and *swam* are verbs in the past tense.

When we ask for A PLACE, we mean any sort of place: a country or city (*Spain, Cleveland*) or a room (*bathroom, kitchen*).

An EXCLAMATION or SILLY WORD is any sort of funny sound, gasp, grunt, or outcry, like *Wow!, Ouch!, Whomp!, Ick!,* and *Gadzooks!*

When we ask for specific words, like a NUMBER, a COLOR, an ANIMAL, or a PART OF THE BODY, we mean a word that is one of those things, like *seven, blue, horse,* or *head.*

When we ask for a PLURAL, it means more than one. For example, *cat* pluralized is *cats.*

VALENTINE'S DAY
MAD LIBS

by Dan Alleva

MAD LIBS® is fun to play with friends, but you can also play it by yourself! To begin with, DO NOT look at the story on the page below. Fill in the blanks on this page with the words called for. Then, using the words you have selected, fill in the blank spaces in the story.

Now you've created your own hilarious MAD LIBS® game!

WHATEVER YOU DO, DON'T FORGET!

ADJECTIVE _____

NUMBER _____

NOUN _____

EXCLAMATION _____

NOUN _____

PERSON IN ROOM _____

ADJECTIVE _____

ANIMAL _____

NOUN _____

PART OF THE BODY _____

TYPE OF FOOD _____

ADJECTIVE _____

A PLACE _____

PLURAL NOUN _____

ADJECTIVE _____

NUMBER _____

ADJECTIVE _____

MAD☺LIBS®
WHATEVER YOU DO, DON'T FORGET!

Ralph never forgets Valentine's Day, and that's for a/an _____

ADJECTIVE

reason. About _____ years ago, Ralph woke up with a terrible

NUMBER

_____ , shouting, "_____!" He had forgotten it

NOUN EXCLAMATION

was Valentine's _____! He knew that his girlfriend,

NOUN

_____ , would be _____ once she found out Ralph

PERSON IN ROOM ADJECTIVE

had forgotten. Ralph leaped out of bed like a/an _____ and

ANIMAL

called his favorite restaurant on the phone. It was going to take a/an

_____ to get a reservation so late. "Are you out of your

NOUN

_____?" the restaurant hostess asked Ralph. "Today is

PART OF THE BODY

Valentine's Day! We've got the best _____ in the city and

TYPE OF FOOD

people have been calling for weeks!" Ralph hung up the phone feeling

_____. "Oh well," he said. "I better go to (the) _____

ADJECTIVE A PLACE

to buy my girlfriend some _____. She'll love them!"

PLURAL NOUN

Unfortunately, Ralph's girlfriend did not love his _____ gifts.

ADJECTIVE

The couple broke up _____ days later. And that was the last time

NUMBER

_____ Ralph forgot about Valentine's Day.

ADJECTIVE

MAD LIBS® is fun to play with friends, but you can also play it by yourself! To begin with, DO NOT look at the story on the page below. Fill in the blanks on this page with the words called for. Then, using the words you have selected, fill in the blank spaces in the story.

Now you've created your own hilarious MAD LIBS® game!

THE ROMANTIC GETAWAY

ADJECTIVE _____

CELEBRITY _____

ADJECTIVE _____

VERB _____

ADJECTIVE _____

ADVERB _____

TYPE OF LIQUID _____

PART OF THE BODY (PLURAL) _____

VERB _____

OCCUPATION _____

ADJECTIVE _____

TYPE OF FOOD _____

TYPE OF FOOD (PLURAL) _____

ADJECTIVE _____

NUMBER _____

TYPE OF FOOD (PLURAL) _____

MAD☺LIBS®

THE ROMANTIC GETAWAY

Are you looking for a/an _____ getaway this Valentine's Day?

ADJECTIVE

If so, you need to visit the _____ Resort and Restaurant!

CELEBRITY

Once you arrive, you'll be greeted in the most _____ way

ADJECTIVE

possible by our welcoming committee. Our goal is to make you

_____ like you're part of our family. And if your luggage is too

VERB

_____ , a member of our staff will _____ bring it to

ADJECTIVE ADVERB

your suite for you! When you arrive at your suite, you will find a

complimentary bottle of _____ on ice. Feel free to have a

TYPE OF LIQUID

drink, kick up your _____ , and relax. Remember,

PART OF THE BODY (PLURAL)

this is your getaway, so there's no need to _____! Next, our

VERB

award-winning _____ has prepared a/an _____

OCCUPATION ADJECTIVE

menu that is just bursting with romance. First up is the _____

TYPE OF FOOD

soup, which will be followed by a delicious salad made from fresh

_____ . For our _____ course, we'll be

TYPE OF FOOD (PLURAL) ADJECTIVE

serving filet mignon! But wait, there's more—for an additional

_____ dollars, you can add romantic chocolate-covered

NUMBER

_____ to your meal. Bon appétit!

TYPE OF FOOD (PLURAL)

MAD LIBS® is fun to play with friends, but you can also play it by yourself! To begin with, DO NOT look at the story on the page below. Fill in the blanks on this page with the words called for. Then, using the words you have selected, fill in the blank spaces in the story.

Now you've created your own hilarious MAD LIBS® game!

A VALENTINE'S PROPOSAL CHECKLIST

PART OF THE BODY _____

ADJECTIVE _____

ADJECTIVE _____

ADJECTIVE _____

PART OF THE BODY _____

ADJECTIVE _____

CELEBRITY _____

NUMBER _____

NOUN _____

OCCUPATION _____

PERSON IN ROOM _____

PART OF THE BODY _____

MAD☺LIBS®
A VALENTINE'S
PROPOSAL CHECKLIST

Are you proposing to your sweet- _____ this Valentine's Day?
PART OF THE BODY

Here are some _____ tips:
ADJECTIVE

1. Don't lose the ring! If you take it out to show your _____
ADJECTIVE

   friend, remember to put it back in your pocket.

2. It is _____ to know your true love's ring size. When you
ADJECTIVE

   propose, you want the ring to fit on their _____ like
PART OF THE BODY

   a glove!

3. Pick the most _____ moment to propose. For example,
ADJECTIVE

   going to see _____ in concert is too noisy. A romantic
CELEBRITY

   dinner for _____ is the perfect moment.
NUMBER

4. If you're having second thoughts about getting married, ask a

   friend or family member for their _____. You can always
NOUN

   talk to a/an _____ for professional advice.
OCCUPATION

5. Be sure to talk to _____ before proposing. Don't
PERSON IN ROOM

   start off on the wrong _____ with your soon-to-be
PART OF THE BODY

   in-laws!

MAD LIBS® is fun to play with friends, but you can also play it by yourself! To begin with, DO NOT look at the story on the page below. Fill in the blanks on this page with the words called for. Then, using the words you have selected, fill in the blank spaces in the story.

Now you've created your own hilarious MAD LIBS® game!

CONVERSATION HEARTS

ADJECTIVE _____

VERB _____

PART OF THE BODY _____

ADJECTIVE _____

VERB _____

ADJECTIVE _____

NOUN _____

NOUN _____

VERB _____

NOUN _____

ADJECTIVE _____

PART OF THE BODY _____

ARTICLE OF CLOTHING (PLURAL) _____

MAD LIBS®

CONVERSATION HEARTS

Giving candy hearts on Valentine's Day is the most _____ way
ADJECTIVE

to say "I _____ you," especially if your honey has a sweet
VERB

_____! Here are some _____ candy sayings that'll
PART OF THE BODY   ADJECTIVE

make anyone _____ madly in love:
VERB

1. I'm _____ about you!
    ADJECTIVE

2. You're my soul _____.
    NOUN

3. Hey there, hot _____!
    NOUN

4. Will you _____ my valentine?
    VERB

5. You're one foxy _____!
    NOUN

6. You drive me _____!
    ADJECTIVE

7. My _____ aches for you!
    PART OF THE BODY

8. You knock my _____ off!
    ARTICLE OF CLOTHING (PLURAL)

MAD LIBS® is fun to play with friends, but you can also play it by yourself! To begin with, DO NOT look at the story on the page below. Fill in the blanks on this page with the words called for. Then, using the words you have selected, fill in the blank spaces in the story.

Now you've created your own hilarious MAD LIBS® game!

A POEM FOR CUPID

VERB _____

ADJECTIVE _____

ADJECTIVE _____

ADVERB _____

TYPE OF FOOD _____

NOUN _____

VERB _____

NOUN _____

NOUN _____

A PLACE _____

VERB _____

PART OF THE BODY _____

VERB _____

ADJECTIVE _____

MAD LIBS

A POEM FOR CUPID

Cupid! Oh, Cupid! I must _____ my match.
                              VERB

I'm _____ , and _____ , and a pretty great catch!
         ADJECTIVE   ADJECTIVE

I went on some dates, but they all were _____ bad.
                                              ADVERB

One date smelled like _____ , one looked like my dad.
                          TYPE OF FOOD

I long for a/an _____ who can match my desire—
                     NOUN

who won't _____ my car or set my _____ on fire.
               VERB   NOUN

I dream of a/an _____ who will call me their honey,
                     NOUN

and take me to (the) _____ ,
                         A PLACE

and won't _____ all my money.
               VERB

Cupid! Oh, Cupid! Am I asking too much?

My _____ has been broken—I'm so out of touch.
    PART OF THE BODY

I wrote you this poem so you'll _____ my plea:
                                      VERB

Please go find a/an _____ match for me!
                        ADJECTIVE

MAD LIBS® is fun to play with friends, but you can also play it by yourself! To begin with, DO NOT look at the story on the page below. Fill in the blanks on this page with the words called for. Then, using the words you have selected, fill in the blank spaces in the story.

Now you've created your own hilarious MAD LIBS® game!

THE FIRST TIME WE MET

PERSON IN ROOM _____

NOUN _____

TYPE OF FOOD (PLURAL) _____

ADJECTIVE _____

ADJECTIVE _____

ARTICLE OF CLOTHING _____

COLOR _____

ADJECTIVE _____

NOUN _____

ADJECTIVE _____

PART OF THE BODY (PLURAL) _____

NOUN _____

VERB _____

TYPE OF FOOD _____

MAD LIBS®

THE FIRST TIME WE MET

My darling _____! I remember the time we first met like it
          PERSON IN ROOM

was _____. We were both standing at the lunch counter
    NOUN

waiting to order _____ when I saw you looking
       TYPE OF FOOD (PLURAL)

_____. I remember thinking, "That is one _____
ADJECTIVE   *ADJECTIVE*

person!" You were wearing a/an _____ and a pair of
                            ARTICLE OF CLOTHING

_____ sunglasses that made you look really _____.
COLOR   *ADJECTIVE*

I ordered my food and returned to my table. Then you approached

and asked, "Is this _____ taken?" You've always had the most
                NOUN

_____ way with words, my love. Then you sat down beside
ADJECTIVE

me, and our _____ locked. It was love at first
            PART OF THE BODY (PLURAL)

_____! My darling, I loved you then as I _____ you
NOUN   *VERB*

now. You will forever be the _____ of my eye!
                         TYPE OF FOOD

MAD LIBS® is fun to play with friends, but you can also play it by yourself! To begin with, DO NOT look at the story on the page below. Fill in the blanks on this page with the words called for. Then, using the words you have selected, fill in the blank spaces in the story.

Now you've created your own hilarious MAD LIBS® game!

A VALENTINE'S DAY PEP TALK

PERSON IN ROOM _____

ADJECTIVE _____

PART OF THE BODY _____

PLURAL NOUN _____

TYPE OF FOOD (PLURAL) _____

PART OF THE BODY _____

ADJECTIVE _____

ADJECTIVE _____

OCCUPATION _____

TYPE OF FOOD (PLURAL) _____

TYPE OF FOOD (PLURAL) _____

ADJECTIVE _____

PLURAL NOUN _____

VERB ENDING IN "ING" _____

ADJECTIVE _____

ADJECTIVE _____

MAD☺LIBS®
A VALENTINE'S DAY
PEP TALK

Let's face it, _____. You've been slacking when it comes to
PERSON IN ROOM

making _____ Valentine's Day plans. We all know that
ADJECTIVE

Valentine's Day can be a royal pain in the _____. And we
PART OF THE BODY

know that corporations use this holiday to make money by selling

greeting _____ and boxes of _____. But
PLURAL NOUN   TYPE OF FOOD (PLURAL)

you still need to get your _____ in the game and make
PART OF THE BODY

_____ plans for your true love! For example, try cooking a/an
ADJECTIVE

_____ meal together to show how much you care. You don't
ADJECTIVE

need to be a master _____ to prepare a delicious meal of
OCCUPATION

pasta, _____, and _____. Also,
TYPE OF FOOD (PLURAL)   TYPE OF FOOD (PLURAL)

you need to get _____ when it comes to choosing gifts.
ADJECTIVE

Instead of giving flowers, try giving _____. And instead
PLURAL NOUN

of _____ the same boring card each year, write
VERB ENDING IN "ING"

your loved one a/an _____ poem! If you try some of these
ADJECTIVE

ideas, you'll have the most _____ Valentine's Day yet.
ADJECTIVE

MAD LIBS® is fun to play with friends, but you can also play it by yourself! To begin with, DO NOT look at the story on the page below. Fill in the blanks on this page with the words called for. Then, using the words you have selected, fill in the blank spaces in the story.

Now you've created your own hilarious MAD LIBS® game!

DATING A MUSICIAN

PART OF THE BODY _____

ADJECTIVE _____

COLOR _____

ANIMAL (PLURAL) _____

VERB _____

NOUN _____

ADJECTIVE _____

PART OF THE BODY (PLURAL) _____

VEHICLE _____

A PLACE _____

ADJECTIVE _____

PLURAL NOUN _____

TYPE OF FOOD _____

NOUN _____

OCCUPATION _____

MAD LIBS®

DATING A MUSICIAN

When it comes to Valentine's Day, my boyfriend and I don't see eye to

_____ . He's a guitar player in a very _____ band,
<u>PART OF THE BODY</u>   <u>ADJECTIVE</u>

the _____ _____ , and he always has to
        <u>COLOR</u>   <u>ANIMAL (PLURAL)</u>

_____ a concert on Valentine's Day. As you can guess, it's not
  <u>VERB</u>

the most romantic place to be with your one true _____ . For
                                                        <u>NOUN</u>

starters, I don't like _____ music, so I always have to wear
                              <u>ADJECTIVE</u>

earplugs in my sensitive _____ . We always ride in
                                  <u>PART OF THE BODY (PLURAL)</u>

the band's official _____ when traveling to (the)
                              <u>VEHICLE</u>

_____ and let me tell you—that ride is absolutely
        <u>A PLACE</u>

_____ and full of trash and _____! And did I
<u>ADJECTIVE</u>   <u>PLURAL NOUN</u>

mention their drummer smells like _____? Touring with a
                                      <u>TYPE OF FOOD</u>

band on Valentine's Day is as romantic as a box of _____ .
                                                           <u>NOUN</u>

Oh well. I guess if I'm not up for the adventure, I should consider

dating a/an _____ instead.
               <u>OCCUPATION</u>

MAD LIBS® is fun to play with friends, but you can also play it by yourself! To begin with, DO NOT look at the story on the page below. Fill in the blanks on this page with the words called for. Then, using the words you have selected, fill in the blank spaces in the story.

Now you've created your own hilarious MAD LIBS® game!

A VALENTINE'S SNOW DAY

ADJECTIVE _____

ANIMAL (PLURAL) _____

PLURAL NOUN _____

NOUN _____

ADJECTIVE _____

TYPE OF LIQUID _____

ADJECTIVE _____

VERB ENDING IN "ING" _____

ARTICLE OF CLOTHING (PLURAL) _____

ADJECTIVE _____

ADJECTIVE _____

ADJECTIVE _____

VERB _____

VERB _____

ADJECTIVE _____

MAD☺LIBS®

A VALENTINE'S SNOW DAY

Nothing puts the fire out on Valentine's Day like a/an _____
ADJECTIVE

blizzard! Here are some ideas for love- _____ who are
ANIMAL (PLURAL)

stuck indoors on a snowy day:

- Grab your _____ and start shoveling that snow!
  PLURAL NOUN

  Teamwork makes the _____ work!
  NOUN

- Get _____ on the sofa together and warm up with a hot
  ADJECTIVE

  cup of _____!
  TYPE OF LIQUID

- Prove you're a/an _____ team by _____
  ADJECTIVE   VERB ENDING IN "ING"

  a puzzle together.

- Spend the day in your _____ surfing the
  ARTICLE OF CLOTHING (PLURAL)

  Internet. Binge-watch a/an _____ TV show together.
  ADJECTIVE

- Bust out your yoga mats and work on your form. After all, practice

  makes _____!
  ADJECTIVE

- Get _____ in the kitchen—find a new recipe and
  ADJECTIVE

  _____ together.
  VERB

- _____ a book to each other—start with a romance novel
  VERB

  or a/an _____ mystery.
  ADJECTIVE

MAD LIBS® is fun to play with friends, but you can also play it by yourself! To begin with, DO NOT look at the story on the page below. Fill in the blanks on this page with the words called for. Then, using the words you have selected, fill in the blank spaces in the story.

Now you've created your own hilarious MAD LIBS® game!

A NOT-SO-SECRET ADMIRER

PERSON IN ROOM _____

ADJECTIVE _____

ADJECTIVE _____

ADJECTIVE _____

VERB _____

ADJECTIVE _____

NUMBER _____

NOUN _____

EXCLAMATION _____

ANIMAL _____

ADJECTIVE _____

FIRST NAME _____

MAD LIBS

A NOT-SO-SECRET ADMIRER

Dear _____ ,
    PERSON IN ROOM

This is a letter from your _____ admirer. I want to wish
                            ADJECTIVE

you a very _____ Valentine's Day. My affection for you is
           ADJECTIVE

_____ , but I'm too scared to _____ you who I am.
ADJECTIVE   VERB

Maybe one day I'll be _____ enough to tell you the truth, but
                    ADJECTIVE

right now I'm not cool enough. Speaking of cool, I saw you got a/an

_____ on last week's exam. Great job! I mean . . . it's not like I sit
NUMBER

behind you in _____ class or anything . . . _____!
           NOUN   EXCLAMATION

Looks like I let the _____ out of the bag. I guess there's no
               ANIMAL

point in keeping my _____ love a secret anymore.
              ADJECTIVE

Will you be my valentine?

Yours truly,

_____
  FIRST NAME

MAD LIBS® is fun to play with friends, but you can also play it by yourself! To begin with, DO NOT look at the story on the page below. Fill in the blanks on this page with the words called for. Then, using the words you have selected, fill in the blank spaces in the story.

Now you've created your own hilarious MAD LIBS® game!

IT'S GALENTINE'S DAY!

CELEBRITY _____

VERB ENDING IN "ING" _____

NOUN _____

ADJECTIVE _____

SILLY WORD _____

NOUN _____

NUMBER _____

TYPE OF LIQUID _____

TYPE OF FOOD (PLURAL) _____

ADJECTIVE _____

VERB ENDING IN "ING" _____

NOUN _____

NOUN _____

VERB _____

ADJECTIVE _____

MAD LIBS®

IT'S GALENTINE'S DAY!

Ever since _____ introduced Galentine's Day to the world,
CELEBRITY

my lady friends and I have been _____ together every
VERB ENDING IN "ING"

year. Galentine's Day takes place on February 13—the _____
NOUN

before Valentine's Day. The holiday is meant to celebrate the

_____ friendships that exist between us girls. So, ladies, let
ADJECTIVE

me hear you say _____ , because today is our day! This year,
SILLY WORD

the annual Galentine's Day brunch will be held at my _____ .
NOUN

I've ordered _____ bottles of _____ to drink. I've
NUMBER   TYPE OF LIQUID

also ordered a full spread of _____ for us gals to eat.
TYPE OF FOOD (PLURAL)

After all, no party is _____ without too much food and
ADJECTIVE

drink! But Galentine's Day is about so much more than eating and

_____ . It's about acknowledging the love and
VERB ENDING IN "ING"

_____ that our friends give one another. You know, the more
NOUN

I think about it, I love Galentine's _____ way more than I
NOUN

_____ Valentine's Day! See you _____ ladies at
VERB   ADJECTIVE

brunch!

MAD LIBS® is fun to play with friends, but you can also play it by yourself! To begin with, DO NOT look at the story on the page below. Fill in the blanks on this page with the words called for. Then, using the words you have selected, fill in the blank spaces in the story.

Now you've created your own hilarious MAD LIBS® game!

VALENTINE'S DAY 2249

NOUN _____

PLURAL NOUN _____

ADJECTIVE _____

NUMBER _____

A PLACE _____

ADJECTIVE _____

ADVERB _____

ADJECTIVE _____

ANIMAL (PLURAL) _____

PERSON IN ROOM _____

PART OF THE BODY (PLURAL) _____

VERB ENDING IN "ING" _____

SILLY WORD _____

ADJECTIVE _____

ADJECTIVE _____

NOUN _____

NOUN _____

MAD LIBS®

VALENTINE'S DAY 2249

The year is 2249 and Earth is no longer the _____ that we
NOUN

remember. The planet has been inhabited by a group of highly

intelligent alien _____ . Valentine's Day has been outlawed
PLURAL NOUN

on the grounds that it's too _____ . Celebrating Valentine's
ADJECTIVE

Day has been ruled a crime, punishable by up to _____ years in
NUMBER

(the) _____ . But there is some _____ news on the
A PLACE   ADJECTIVE

horizon. A rebel group is _____ hiding in the shadows,
ADVERB

planning an uprising against the _____ alien dictators. The
ADJECTIVE

group is called the Love _____ , and their leader goes
ANIMAL (PLURAL)

by the name of _____ . Any hope of returning love to Earth
PERSON IN ROOM

lies in their capable _____ . The enemy is
PART OF THE BODY (PLURAL)

_____ stronger every day, especially since acquiring
VERB ENDING IN "ING"

_____—a/an _____ energy source with the
SILLY WORD   ADJECTIVE

capability to destroy _____ love in seconds. As the fate of
ADJECTIVE

humanity hangs by a/an _____ , the citizens of Earth hold
NOUN

their breath. Good luck, rebels. You'll need all the _____ you
NOUN

can get.

MAD LIBS® is fun to play with friends, but you can also play it by yourself! To begin with, DO NOT look at the story on the page below. Fill in the blanks on this page with the words called for. Then, using the words you have selected, fill in the blank spaces in the story.

Now you've created your own hilarious MAD LIBS® game!

THE HIGH-SCHOOL VALENTINE'S DAY DANCE

ADJECTIVE _____

ADJECTIVE _____

FIRST NAME _____

VERB _____

VERB _____

NUMBER _____

NUMBER _____

NOUN _____

CELEBRITY _____

SILLY WORD _____

ANIMAL _____

VERB ENDING IN "ING" _____

PART OF THE BODY _____

ADJECTIVE _____

ADJECTIVE _____

VERB ENDING IN "ING" _____

VERB _____

ADJECTIVE _____

MAD☺LIBS®
THE HIGH-SCHOOL
VALENTINE'S DAY DANCE

As your father, I'm so _____ that you're finally going to your
                  ADJECTIVE

first Valentine's Day dance. It's a/an _____ rite of passage
                            ADJECTIVE

that you'll always remember. Now, the most important thing,

_____ , is not to be nervous. This night should be fun, so
FIRST NAME

don't _____—everything is going to be great! I'll never
       VERB

_____ my first time at a Valentine's Day dance. It was
VERB

_____ years ago. I wasn't much older than you are now,
NUMBER

though you're about _____ inches taller than I was back
                NUMBER

then. I was the shortest _____ in my class! But the one
                   NOUN

thing I could do really well was dance like _____ . I knew all
                      CELEBRITY

the popular steps of my day—the _____ , the Funky
                     SILLY WORD

_____ , and the _____ Man. I could
ANIMAL   VERB ENDING IN "ING"

really shake my _____ with the best of them! That night,
         PART OF THE BODY

I danced with the most _____ girl in school. She was a/an
                ADJECTIVE

_____ dancer, too. It was as if we were _____
ADJECTIVE   VERB ENDING IN "ING"

on air together. And if you don't believe me, just _____ your
                    VERB

mother. She was the _____ girl who danced with me!
          ADJECTIVE

MAD LIBS® is fun to play with friends, but you can also play it by yourself! To begin with, DO NOT look at the story on the page below. Fill in the blanks on this page with the words called for. Then, using the words you have selected, fill in the blank spaces in the story.

Now you've created your own hilarious MAD LIBS® game!

MY CRUMMY VALENTINE'S

ADVERB _____

ANIMAL (PLURAL) _____

ANIMAL (PLURAL) _____

PART OF THE BODY (PLURAL) _____

NUMBER _____

VERB _____

ADJECTIVE _____

SILLY WORD _____

VERB _____

ARTICLE OF CLOTHING (PLURAL) _____

NOUN _____

PLURAL NOUN _____

ADJECTIVE _____

A PLACE _____

TYPE OF FOOD _____

ANIMAL _____

VERB _____

MAD LIBS

MY CRUMMY VALENTINE'S

This Valentine's Day was _____ the worst one I've ever had!
ADVERB

It was raining _____ and _____ when I
ANIMAL (PLURAL)   ANIMAL (PLURAL)

rushed to the bus, already late for school. I was soaked all the way from

my head to my _____ . I was _____ minutes
PART OF THE BODY (PLURAL)   NUMBER

late for first period, so I tried to _____ into the room without
VERB

being seen. Unfortunately, there was already a/an _____ quiz
ADJECTIVE

waiting for me on my desk. "_____ ," I muttered to myself,
SILLY WORD

trying to _____ the assignment. By the afternoon, my
VERB

_____ had dried, but my day hadn't gotten
ARTICLE OF CLOTHING (PLURAL)

any better! In _____ class, the teacher yelled at me for being
NOUN

late again—in front of all my _____ . Then someone ate
PLURAL NOUN

the _____ lunch I had brought from (the) _____ . It
ADJECTIVE   A PLACE

was my favorite—a ham and _____ sandwich. What is wrong
TYPE OF FOOD

with people?! So, there I was on Valentine's Day: wet, embarrassed, and

hungry enough to eat a/an _____ ! I guess not even true love
ANIMAL

could _____ this terrible day.
VERB

MAD LIBS® is fun to play with friends, but you can also play it by yourself! To begin with, DO NOT look at the story on the page below. Fill in the blanks on this page with the words called for. Then, using the words you have selected, fill in the blank spaces in the story.

Now you've created your own hilarious MAD LIBS® game!

THE VALENTINE'S DAY SCAVENGER HUNT

FIRST NAME _____

ADJECTIVE _____

ADJECTIVE _____

A PLACE _____

NOUN _____

COLOR _____

CELEBRITY _____

NUMBER _____

NOUN _____

VERB _____

COLOR _____

PERSON IN ROOM _____

PLURAL NOUN _____

TYPE OF FOOD _____

TYPE OF LIQUID _____

PERSON IN ROOM _____

MAD LIBS®
THE VALENTINE'S DAY
SCAVENGER HUNT

Dear _____ ,
　　　　　FIRST NAME

This year I thought we'd do something a little _____ for
　　　　　　　　　　　　　　　　　　　　　　　ADJECTIVE

Valentine's Day. I've arranged a/an _____ scavenger hunt!
　　　　　　　　　　　　　　　　ADJECTIVE

First, you need to go to (the) _____ . Underneath the
　　　　　　　　　　　　　　　　A PLACE

_____ , you'll find a/an _____ envelope with a key.
NOUN　　　　　　　　　　　　COLOR

Take the key, walk to _____ Towers downtown, and climb
　　　　　　　　　　　CELEBRITY

_____ floors to a jazz club. There, you'll find a woman playing
NUMBER

the _____ . Once she finishes her song, _____ her
　　NOUN　　　　　　　　　　　　　　　　　　VERB

for your next clue and she'll hand you a/an _____ envelope.
　　　　　　　　　　　　　　　　　　　COLOR

This one will have a picture of _____ 's Café—the spot where
　　　　　　　　　　　　PERSON IN ROOM

we first met. When you arrive at the café, tell the barista, "I'm just here

for the _____ ." The barista will reveal a secret location
　　　　PLURAL NOUN

where I'll be waiting for you with roses and a box of _____ .
　　　　　　　　　　　　　　　　　　　　　　　TYPE OF FOOD

I can't wait to see you! Oh, and since you'll be coming from the café,

could you bring me a cup of _____ ?
　　　　　　　　　　　　　TYPE OF LIQUID

All my love,

_____
PERSON IN ROOM

MAD LIBS® is fun to play with friends, but you can also play it by yourself! To begin with, DO NOT look at the story on the page below. Fill in the blanks on this page with the words called for. Then, using the words you have selected, fill in the blank spaces in the story.

Now you've created your own hilarious MAD LIBS® game!

A VALENTINE'S DAY BIRTHDAY

VERB _____

NUMBER _____

PLURAL NOUN _____

TYPE OF FOOD _____

COLOR _____

PLURAL NOUN _____

VERB ENDING IN "ING" _____

ADJECTIVE _____

ADJECTIVE _____

ADJECTIVE _____

ADJECTIVE _____

NOUN _____

VERB _____

NOUN _____

ADJECTIVE _____

NUMBER _____

ARTICLE OF CLOTHING (PLURAL) _____

MAD LIBS
A VALENTINE'S DAY
BIRTHDAY

When people complain about having a birthday on Christmas, it

makes me want to _____! A Valentine's Day birthday is
                    VERB

_____ times worse—and I have the _____ to prove
  NUMBER   PLURAL NOUN

it. First, my friends always buy me romantic gifts like candy hearts,

_____ truffles, and _____ roses. I know it's only
  TYPE OF FOOD   COLOR

because those _____ are on sale. People do the same thing
               PLURAL NOUN

with _____ cards, too. Last year, my _____
     VERB ENDING IN "ING"   ADJECTIVE

friend gave me a card that read "_____ Valentine's Day" on the
                                   ADJECTIVE

front. Inside, she wrote "And _____ birthday, too." I mean, is
                              ADJECTIVE

it too _____ to buy the right card? Finally, no one ever wants
        ADJECTIVE

to party with their friends on Valentine's _____. My friends
                                            NOUN

all want to kiss and _____ their partners instead. Everyone
                     VERB

tells me I'm acting like a spoiled _____. But it's very
                                    NOUN

_____ to have a birthday on Valentine's Day! Unless you've
  ADJECTIVE

walked _____ miles in my _____, you
        NUMBER   ARTICLE OF CLOTHING (PLURAL)

wouldn't understand.

MAD LIBS® is fun to play with friends, but you can also play it by yourself! To begin with, DO NOT look at the story on the page below. Fill in the blanks on this page with the words called for. Then, using the words you have selected, fill in the blank spaces in the story.

Now you've created your own hilarious MAD LIBS® game!

VALENTINE'S DAY FROM A FARAWAY PLACE

PERSON IN ROOM _____

ADJECTIVE _____

COUNTRY _____

ADJECTIVE _____

PART OF THE BODY _____

LETTER OF THE ALPHABET _____

NUMBER _____

ADJECTIVE _____

VEHICLE _____

ADJECTIVE _____

TYPE OF FOOD (PLURAL) _____

TYPE OF FOOD (PLURAL) _____

VERB ENDING IN "ING" _____

PART OF THE BODY _____

ADJECTIVE _____

ADJECTIVE _____

PERSON IN ROOM _____

MAD LIBS®
VALENTINE'S DAY FROM
A FARAWAY PLACE

Dearest _____,
         PERSON IN ROOM

I hope this e-mail finds you in a/an _____ mood! My flight to
                                        ADJECTIVE

_____ landed not too long ago. I hate being far away from
     COUNTRY

my one _____ love on Valentine's Day, but distance makes the
       ADJECTIVE

_____ grow fonder. My flight was supposed to arrive
PART OF THE BODY

at Gate _____ almost _____ hours ago.
        LETTER OF THE ALPHABET   NUMBER

Unfortunately, there were _____ delays. By the time they let
                              ADJECTIVE

us off the _____ , I was starving! I found a very _____
            VEHICLE   ADJECTIVE

café near the airport and ate a burger, _____,
                                          TYPE OF FOOD (PLURAL)

and some _____. Now I'm at the hotel,
           TYPE OF FOOD (PLURAL)

_____ this letter to you and wishing I could hold your
VERB ENDING IN "ING"

beautiful _____ in my hands. Anyway, I'm really
          PART OF THE BODY

_____ after that flight, so I'm going to bed. I promise to have
ADJECTIVE

the most _____ dreams of you. Happy Valentine's Day!
         ADJECTIVE

All my love,

_____
PERSON IN ROOM

MAD LIBS® is fun to play with friends, but you can also play it by yourself! To begin with, DO NOT look at the story on the page below. Fill in the blanks on this page with the words called for. Then, using the words you have selected, fill in the blank spaces in the story.

Now you've created your own hilarious MAD LIBS® game!

ROSES ARE RED, VIOLETS ARE BLUE

COLOR _____

TYPE OF FOOD _____

ADJECTIVE _____

VERB _____

VERB _____

ADJECTIVE _____

PART OF THE BODY _____

COLOR _____

PLURAL NOUN _____

COLOR _____

PLURAL NOUN _____

ADJECTIVE _____

MAD LIBS
ROSES ARE RED,
VIOLETS ARE BLUE

Roses are _____ , violets are blue,
COLOR

_____ is _____ , and darling, so are you.
TYPE OF FOOD   ADJECTIVE

I will be yours and you will be mine.

The love that we _____ is mighty fine.
VERB

We help each other in all sorts of ways.

I hope I can _____ you for all of my days.
VERB

Your _____ smile is all that I need.
ADJECTIVE

I'll take your _____ and I'll follow your lead.
PART OF THE BODY

Your lush _____ hair complements your eyes,
COLOR

which shine like _____ above in the skies.
PLURAL NOUN

So, roses are _____ , and violets are blue,
COLOR

but I know you like daisies and _____ , too.
PLURAL NOUN

Let's end this poem, and all I will say

is "I hope you have a very _____ Valentine's Day!"
ADJECTIVE

MAD LIBS® is fun to play with friends, but you can also play it by yourself! To begin with, DO NOT look at the story on the page below. Fill in the blanks on this page with the words called for. Then, using the words you have selected, fill in the blank spaces in the story.

Now you've created your own hilarious MAD LIBS® game!

I LOVE YOU A LATTE, MOM

ADJECTIVE _____

ADJECTIVE _____

ARTICLE OF CLOTHING _____

VERB _____

VERB _____

A PLACE _____

ADJECTIVE _____

ADJECTIVE _____

COUNTRY _____

TYPE OF FOOD _____

ADJECTIVE _____

TYPE OF FOOD (PLURAL) _____

PLURAL NOUN _____

ADVERB _____

ADJECTIVE _____

EXCLAMATION _____

NOUN _____

MAD LIBS®

I LOVE YOU A LATTE, MOM

My mom loves the _____ taste of coffee. She loves it so much
　　　　　　　　　　ADJECTIVE

it's kind of _____! She even has a/an _____
　　　　　　　ADJECTIVE　　　　　　　　　　　　　　　ARTICLE OF CLOTHING

that reads "Don't _____ Me Until I've Had My Coffee."
　　　　　　　　　　　　VERB

When she sees what I bought her for Valentine's Day, she's going to

_____ out! I went to (the) _____ near our house and
　　VERB　　　　　　　　　　　　　　　　A PLACE

bought the most _____ coffee they sell. The _____
　　　　　　　　　ADJECTIVE　　　　　　　　　　　　　　　　ADJECTIVE

woman in the store said the coffee beans were grown in _____
　　　　　　　　　　　　　　　　　　　　　　　　　　　　　　　COUNTRY

and had hints of toffee, hazelnut, and _____. I can't wait to
　　　　　　　　　　　　　　　　　　　　TYPE OF FOOD

give her my gift! It's going to be so much better than my dad's

_____ present. He always gets her chocolate-covered
ADJECTIVE

_____ and a bouquet of _____. But
TYPE OF FOOD (PLURAL)　　　　　　　　　　　　　PLURAL NOUN

those gifts are _____ boring. These days, you need to be
　　　　　　　　　　ADVERB

_____ when it comes to gift giving. You need a gift that makes
ADJECTIVE

the recipient say, "_____!" I love my mom and she
　　　　　　　　　　　EXCLAMATION

deserves the best _____ that money can buy!
　　　　　　　　　　　　NOUN

MAD LIBS® is fun to play with friends, but you can also play it by yourself! To begin with, DO NOT look at the story on the page below. Fill in the blanks on this page with the words called for. Then, using the words you have selected, fill in the blank spaces in the story.

Now you've created your own hilarious MAD LIBS® game!

FIRST CRUSH

ADJECTIVE _____

PERSON IN ROOM _____

COLOR _____

NOUN _____

ADVERB _____

ADJECTIVE _____

NOUN _____

PLURAL NOUN _____

PART OF THE BODY _____

NUMBER _____

VERB _____

NOUN _____

NOUN _____

VERB _____

VERB _____

NUMBER _____

NOUN _____

MAD LIBS

FIRST CRUSH

I still remember my first crush back when I was a/an _____
ADJECTIVE

kid. His name was _____ and he was a cute, tall,
PERSON IN ROOM

_____-haired boy from my school. I sat behind him in
COLOR

_____ class, but he _____ noticed me at all. You see,
NOUN   ADVERB

he was _____ and popular, while I was kind of a/an
ADJECTIVE

_____. He played lacrosse, while I played Dungeons &
NOUN

_____. Still, my _____ would grow _____
PLURAL NOUN   PART OF THE BODY   NUMBER

times bigger when I saw him. One Valentine's Day, I decided to

_____ him a love letter. I poured my heart into that letter
VERB

and then I slipped the _____ into his locker. I hid behind a
NOUN

trash can as he opened his _____ and started reading my
NOUN

note. I thought I was going to _____ , I was so nervous! That's
VERB

when I realized—I forgot to _____ my name on the letter.
VERB

Even though it was _____ years ago, I guess I'll always be his
NUMBER

secret _____ !
NOUN

From VALENTINE'S DAY MAD LIBS® • Copyright © 2019 by Penguin Random House LLC.

MAD LIBS® is fun to play with friends, but you can also play it by yourself! To begin with, DO NOT look at the story on the page below. Fill in the blanks on this page with the words called for. Then, using the words you have selected, fill in the blank spaces in the story.

Now you've created your own hilarious MAD LIBS® game!

THE HISTORY OF VALENTINE'S DAY

ADJECTIVE _____

OCCUPATION _____

NUMBER _____

ADJECTIVE _____

COUNTRY _____

ADJECTIVE _____

NOUN _____

ADJECTIVE _____

NOUN _____

PLURAL NOUN _____

ADJECTIVE _____

VERB (PAST TENSE) _____

VERB _____

NOUN _____

ADJECTIVE _____

MAD LIBS®
THE HISTORY OF
VALENTINE'S DAY

Do you know the _____ history of Valentine's Day? There are
                        ADJECTIVE

many different legends about St. Valentine, but scholars believe he was

a/an _____ who lived in Rome around AD _____.
        OCCUPATION   NUMBER

When St. Valentine was alive, there was a/an _____ war
                                                ADJECTIVE

between Rome and _____. The _____ emperor
                    COUNTRY   ADJECTIVE

of Rome decided that single men made better soldiers than married

men, so he outlawed marriage across the _____. St. Valentine
                                            NOUN

knew this was a/an _____ idea, so he ignored the emperor's
                        ADJECTIVE

_____ and continued to perform marriages for young
    NOUN

_____ in secret. When the emperor found out, he was so
    PLURAL NOUN

_____ that he ordered St. Valentine to be _____!
    ADJECTIVE   VERB (PAST TENSE)

Now on Valentine's Day we _____ St. Valentine's bravery by
                            VERB

celebrating love and _____. So, have a/an _____
                        NOUN   ADJECTIVE

Valentine's Day, everyone!

PEACE, LOVE, AND
MAD LIBS

by Roger Price & Leonard Stern

MAD LIBS® is fun to play with friends, but you can also play it by yourself! To begin with, DO NOT look at the story on the page below. Fill in the blanks on this page with the words called for. Then, using the words you have selected, fill in the blank spaces in the story.

Now you've created your own hilarious MAD LIBS® game!

PEACE IS THE WORD

NOUN _____

NUMBER _____

PLURAL NOUN _____

COLOR _____

NOUN _____

NOUN _____

NOUN _____

PERSON IN ROOM _____

VERB (PAST TENSE) _____

NOUN _____

ADJECTIVE _____

PART OF THE BODY (PLURAL) _____

ADJECTIVE _____

NOUN _____

PLURAL NOUN _____

PLURAL NOUN _____

MAD LIBS®

PEACE IS THE WORD

Our _____ studies teacher had us write a/an
　　　　　　　　NOUN

_____-word paper on the different symbols for peace.
　　NUMBER

I learned many interesting _____ , such as:
　　　　　　　　　　　　　PLURAL NOUN

- The _____ dove is a symbol of love, peace, and
　　　　　COLOR

  _____ .
　　NOUN

- The olive _____ represents a peace offering or goodwill
　　　　　　　NOUN

  gesture, as in: *The next-door neighbors extended a/an* _____
　　　　　　　　　　　　　　　　　　　　　　　　　　　NOUN

  branch to _____ *after their dog* _____ *on*
　　　　　　PERSON IN ROOM　　　　　　　　VERB (PAST TENSE)

  the _____ .
　　　NOUN

- The "V" sign is a/an _____ gesture made by holding up
　　　　　　　　　　　ADJECTIVE

  two _____ in the shape of the letter *V.*
　　PART OF THE BODY (PLURAL)

- The peace sign is one of the most _____ symbols in the
　　　　　　　　　　　　　　　　　ADJECTIVE

  _____ . It was popular with hippies, who spray-painted
　　NOUN

  it on _____ while shouting, "Give _____
　　　PLURAL NOUN　　　　　　　　　　　　　　PLURAL NOUN

  a chance!"

From PEACE, LOVE, AND MAD LIBS® • Copyright © 2009 by Penguin Random House LLC.

MAD LIBS® is fun to play with friends, but you can also play it by yourself! To begin with, DO NOT look at the story on the page below. Fill in the blanks on this page with the words called for. Then, using the words you have selected, fill in the blank spaces in the story.

Now you've created your own hilarious MAD LIBS® game!

THE HIPPIE SHACK

PART OF THE BODY _____

ADJECTIVE _____

NOUN _____

PLURAL NOUN _____

PLURAL NOUN _____

NOUN _____

ARTICLE OF CLOTHING _____

NOUN _____

PART OF THE BODY _____

ADJECTIVE _____

ADJECTIVE _____

NOUN _____

PLURAL NOUN _____

PART OF THE BODY _____

VERB ENDING IN "ING" _____

NOUN _____

ADJECTIVE _____

MAD LIBS®

THE HIPPIE SHACK

Are you a hippie wannabe? If so, visit the Hippie Shack. They'll outfit

you from head to _____ in the _____,
                    PART OF THE BODY   ADJECTIVE

colorful clothing worn by those _____ -loving flower
                                       NOUN

_____ of the '60s! We suggest starting with basic
   PLURAL NOUN

bell-bottom _____ , preferably a vintage pair with
              PLURAL NOUN

_____ -shaped patches sewn over the holes. Then select any
   NOUN

_____ with fringe, tie-dye, or a psychedelic _____
ARTICLE OF CLOTHING   NOUN

pattern. You can accessorize to your _____'s content!
                                       PART OF THE BODY

We have some _____ belts and _____ jewelry
               ADJECTIVE   ADJECTIVE

with the peace _____ displayed. Or you can wear strings
                   NOUN

of beaded _____ , and we have scarves that wrap around
            PLURAL NOUN

your _____ . Trust us, when you step out of the
       PART OF THE BODY

_____ room in your cool new threads, you'll
   VERB ENDING IN "ING"

not only look like a groovy _____ , you'll feel pretty
                               NOUN

_____ , too!
   ADJECTIVE

MAD LIBS® is fun to play with friends, but you can also play it by yourself! To begin with, DO NOT look at the story on the page below. Fill in the blanks on this page with the words called for. Then, using the words you have selected, fill in the blank spaces in the story.

Now you've created your own hilarious MAD LIBS® game!

HAPPENING

VERB _____

NUMBER _____

ADJECTIVE _____

ADJECTIVE _____

NOUN _____

ADJECTIVE _____

PLURAL NOUN _____

A PLACE _____

ADJECTIVE _____

PLURAL NOUN _____

PERSON IN ROOM _____

ANIMAL (PLURAL) _____

VERB ENDING IN "ING" _____

TYPE OF FOOD (PLURAL) _____

NOUN _____

ADJECTIVE _____

NOUN _____

VERB _____

NOUN _____

 MAD LIBS®

HAPPENING

Run, don't _____ , to join _____ of your closest
            VERB   NUMBER

friends at the greatest _____ outdoor musical experience of
                              ADJECTIVE

our _____ generation. This once-in-a/an- _____
      ADJECTIVE   NOUN

event is guaranteed to provide a/an _____ weekend filled
                                    ADJECTIVE

with music, peace, love, and _____ in the picturesque
                              PLURAL NOUN

setting of (the) _____ . Bands such as the _____
               A PLACE   ADJECTIVE

_____ , _____ and the _____ ,
  PLURAL NOUN   PERSON IN ROOM   ANIMAL (PLURAL)

the _____ _____ , and many more
    VERB ENDING IN "ING"   TYPE OF FOOD (PLURAL)

will be rocking the _____ all night long! This _____
               NOUN   ADJECTIVE

happening will take place rain or _____ , so _____
                            NOUN   VERB

accordingly. It's sure to be a legendary _____ !
                                  NOUN

MAD LIBS® is fun to play with friends, but you can also play it by yourself! To begin with, DO NOT look at the story on the page below. Fill in the blanks on this page with the words called for. Then, using the words you have selected, fill in the blank spaces in the story.

Now you've created your own hilarious MAD LIBS® game!

WORLD PEACE... AND OTHER PROMISES

ADJECTIVE _____

PERSON IN ROOM _____

PLURAL NOUN _____

ADVERB _____

ADJECTIVE _____

PLURAL NOUN _____

NOUN _____

PLURAL NOUN _____

TYPE OF LIQUID _____

NOUN _____

ADJECTIVE _____

ADVERB _____

PLURAL NOUN _____

PLURAL NOUN _____

PLURAL NOUN _____

NOUN _____

SAME PERSON IN ROOM _____

ADJECTIVE _____

MAD LIBS®
WORLD PEACE . . .
AND OTHER PROMISES

Our school is voting for this year's _____ president! Let's

ADJECTIVE

listen in as the candidate, _____, makes their final

PERSON IN ROOM

campaign speech:

"My fellow _____: I know the changes you want and

PLURAL NOUN

_____ deserve. If elected, I promise to put an end to

ADVERB

_____ homework and pop _____. I will expand

ADJECTIVE — PLURAL NOUN

the lunch menu to include _____-burgers and cheese-

NOUN

stuffed _____. I will fill every drinking fountain with

PLURAL NOUN

chocolate _____. I will see to it that the only acceptable

TYPE OF LIQUID

exercise in gym class is dodge-_____. Finally, for every

NOUN

_____ student in detention, I _____ swear to

ADJECTIVE — ADVERB

make video _____, comic _____, and

PLURAL NOUN — PLURAL NOUN

widescreen _____ available in the detention _____.

PLURAL NOUN — NOUN

So remember: A vote for _____ today is a vote for

SAME PERSON IN ROOM

a/an _____ school tomorrow!"

ADJECTIVE

MAD LIBS® is fun to play with friends, but you can also play it by yourself! To begin with, DO NOT look at the story on the page below. Fill in the blanks on this page with the words called for. Then, using the words you have selected, fill in the blank spaces in the story.

Now you've created your own hilarious MAD LIBS® game!

HAPPY CAMPERS

ADJECTIVE _____

ADJECTIVE _____

ADJECTIVE _____

PLURAL NOUN _____

PLURAL NOUN _____

ADJECTIVE _____

NOUN _____

VERB ENDING IN "ING" _____

NOUN _____

ARTICLE OF CLOTHING (PLURAL) _____

NOUN _____

TYPE OF FOOD (PLURAL) _____

TYPE OF LIQUID _____

VERB ENDING IN "ING" _____

ADJECTIVE _____

NOUN _____

MAD☺LIBS®

HAPPY CAMPERS

When life gets too _____, there's no better antidote than
                        ADJECTIVE

to forget the _____ grind and go camping with some
                  ADJECTIVE

_____ friends. With the moon and _____
  ADJECTIVE   PLURAL NOUN

twinkling overhead and the sound of _____ chirping
                                        PLURAL NOUN

in the woods, sitting around the campfire and singing a/an

_____ chorus or two of "She'll Be Coming 'Round the
  ADJECTIVE

_____" or "I've Been _____ on the
  NOUN   VERB ENDING IN "ING"

Railroad" is a great way to restore peace to your inner _____.
                                                            NOUN

Or, if you choose, you can scare the _____ off
                                        ARTICLE OF CLOTHING (PLURAL)

everyone with _____ stories. You can also just sit quietly,
                  NOUN

toasting _____ and sipping mugs of steaming
            TYPE OF FOOD (PLURAL)

_____ before snuggling into your _____
  TYPE OF LIQUID   VERB ENDING IN "ING"

bag. Yes, there's nothing better than the _____ outdoors to
                                              ADJECTIVE

guarantee a good night's _____!
                            NOUN

MAD LIBS® is fun to play with friends, but you can also play it by yourself! To begin with, DO NOT look at the story on the page below. Fill in the blanks on this page with the words called for. Then, using the words you have selected, fill in the blank spaces in the story.

Now you've created your own hilarious MAD LIBS® game!

FOR PEACE SAKE!

ADJECTIVE _____

PLURAL NOUN _____

VERB ENDING IN "ING" _____

PART OF THE BODY (PLURAL) _____

NOUN _____

PLURAL NOUN _____

ADVERB _____

NOUN _____

VERB _____

PLURAL NOUN _____

NUMBER _____

PART OF THE BODY (PLURAL) _____

VERB _____

PLURAL NOUN _____

ADJECTIVE _____

NOUN _____

MAD LIBS

FOR PEACE SAKE!

My _____ brother and sister are at it again, fighting like cats
   ADJECTIVE

and _____. I've had enough. I've decided to give them a
   PLURAL NOUN

stern _____-to. I will look them straight in their
   VERB ENDING IN "ING"

_____ and say, "Living under the same
PART OF THE BODY (PLURAL)

_____ means we're going to get on one another's
   NOUN

_____ from time to time, but you two are being
PLURAL NOUN

_____ insensitive! You don't have to argue at the drop of a/an
ADVERB

_____. Think before you _____. Take a few deep
   NOUN   VERB

_____ and count to _____. If you don't, I'm
PLURAL NOUN   NUMBER

warning you, I'll take matters into my own _____
                                           PART OF THE BODY (PLURAL)

and _____ you flat on your _____! Now let's
        VERB   PLURAL NOUN

have some _____ peace and _____."
             ADJECTIVE   NOUN

MAD LIBS® is fun to play with friends, but you can also play it by yourself! To begin with, DO NOT look at the story on the page below. Fill in the blanks on this page with the words called for. Then, using the words you have selected, fill in the blank spaces in the story.

Now you've created your own hilarious MAD LIBS® game!

FAR-OUT FOOD

ADJECTIVE _____

PART OF THE BODY _____

NOUN _____

NUMBER _____

ADJECTIVE _____

ADJECTIVE _____

NOUN _____

ADJECTIVE _____

PLURAL NOUN _____

ADJECTIVE _____

PLURAL NOUN _____

NOUN _____

ADVERB _____

NOUN _____

NOUN _____

PLURAL NOUN _____

PART OF THE BODY _____

ADJECTIVE _____

FAR-OUT FOOD

Welcome to the Far-Out Café! Our _____ diner serves
<small>ADJECTIVE</small>

_____-lickin'-good eats that are out of this _____.
<small>PART OF THE BODY</small>   <small>NOUN</small>

Our most popular dishes are:

- **Hippie Hamburger:** _____ ounces of _____
  <small>NUMBER</small>   <small>ADJECTIVE</small>

  beef on a/an _____ bun, stacked with sprouts, tomato,
  <small>ADJECTIVE</small>

  and a/an _____ slice
  <small>NOUN</small>

- **Flower Child Chicken:** This _____ dish is served with
  <small>ADJECTIVE</small>

  wild _____ and homegrown _____ vegetables
  <small>PLURAL NOUN</small>   <small>ADJECTIVE</small>

  on a bed of flower _____
  <small>PLURAL NOUN</small>

- **Groovy Grilled Cheese:** Sharp _____ cheese melted
  <small>NOUN</small>

  between two slices of _____ baked _____,
  <small>ADVERB</small>   <small>NOUN</small>

  served with _____ chips
  <small>NOUN</small>

- **Psychedelic Salad:** On a bed of dark leafy _____, an
  <small>PLURAL NOUN</small>

  array of creative exuberances that will tempt your _____
  <small>PART OF THE BODY</small>

  and provide a/an _____ meal in itself
  <small>ADJECTIVE</small>

MAD LIBS® is fun to play with friends, but you can also play it by yourself! To begin with, DO NOT look at the story on the page below. Fill in the blanks on this page with the words called for. Then, using the words you have selected, fill in the blank spaces in the story.

Now you've created your own hilarious MAD LIBS® game!

A LITTLE PEACE & QUIET

NOUN _____

NOUN _____

PLURAL NOUN _____

NOUN _____

NOUN _____

PLURAL NOUN _____

NOUN _____

ADVERB _____

PLURAL NOUN _____

PLURAL NOUN _____

PLURAL NOUN _____

PLURAL NOUN _____

PART OF THE BODY (PLURAL) _____

PLURAL NOUN _____

PLURAL NOUN _____

PLURAL NOUN _____

NOUN _____

MAD LIBS

A LITTLE PEACE & QUIET

What would happen if you fell overboard from a/an _____
                                                        NOUN

and washed up on a deserted tropical _____? Here's a list of
                                              NOUN

survival _____:
          PLURAL NOUN

- The human _____ requires one thing more than all
                   NOUN

  others to survive: _____. Without water, you would
                            NOUN

  only last for a few _____. So you'd have to find a source
                           PLURAL NOUN

  of fresh running _____ and boil it before _____
                          NOUN   ADVERB

  drinking it.

- Look for plants, _____, and insects to eat. You can also
                        PLURAL NOUN

  try leaves, berries, and even the bark of some _____.
                                                        PLURAL NOUN

- Food can also be hunted with primitive _____. Use
                                                PLURAL NOUN

  rocks, sticks, ropes, _____, or anything else you can
                             PLURAL NOUN

  get your _____ on.
              PART OF THE BODY (PLURAL)

- Gather _____ for a campfire. Rub two _____
               PLURAL NOUN   PLURAL NOUN

  together until a fire is created. You will have warmth and a way to

  cook and boil your _____. Perhaps most
                            PLURAL NOUN

  importantly, you'll have a way to signal a passing _____.
                                                            NOUN

MAD LIBS® is fun to play with friends, but you can also play it by yourself! To begin with, DO NOT look at the story on the page below. Fill in the blanks on this page with the words called for. Then, using the words you have selected, fill in the blank spaces in the story.

Now you've created your own hilarious MAD LIBS® game!

EVERYONE NEEDS A GOOD FRIEND

ADVERB _____

NOUN _____

ADJECTIVE _____

ADJECTIVE _____

ADJECTIVE _____

PLURAL NOUN _____

COLOR _____

PLURAL NOUN _____

VERB _____

NOUN _____

NOUN _____

PLURAL NOUN _____

MAD☺LIBS®
EVERYONE NEEDS
A GOOD FRIEND

As a Greek philosopher _____ once said, "One good
                              ADVERB

_____ makes a poor man rich." Here are some important
      NOUN

qualities to look for in a/an _____ friend:
                                ADJECTIVE

• Whether you're right or _____ , your friend will be there
                              ADJECTIVE

  for you—through thick and _____ .
                                  ADJECTIVE

• When you are down in the _____ and feeling
                                PLURAL NOUN

  _____ , your friend will tell you funny _____
      COLOR   *PLURAL NOUN*

  to make you _____ with laughter.
                  VERB

• When you don't have a/an _____ to wear, your friend
                              NOUN

  should generously offer you their favorite _____ so you
                                                  NOUN

  can look like a million _____ .
                            PLURAL NOUN

MAD LIBS® is fun to play with friends, but you can also play it by yourself! To begin with, DO NOT look at the story on the page below. Fill in the blanks on this page with the words called for. Then, using the words you have selected, fill in the blank spaces in the story.

Now you've created your own hilarious MAD LIBS® game!

PEACE, LOVE, AND POETRY

PLURAL NOUN _____

PERSON IN ROOM _____

VERB _____

NOUN _____

PLURAL NOUN _____

ADJECTIVE _____

PLURAL NOUN _____

NOUN _____

COLOR _____

PART OF THE BODY _____

VERB _____

NOUN _____

PLURAL NOUN _____

ADVERB _____

A PLACE _____

MAD LIBS

PEACE, LOVE, AND POETRY

"Peace, Love, and the Pursuit of _____"
                                   PLURAL NOUN

by _____
   PERSON IN ROOM

Teach everyone you meet to _____ in perfect harmony,
                                VERB

reach out and embrace a friend or _____, or go hug a tree!
                                        NOUN

Preach to _____, both big and _____,
           PLURAL NOUN   ADJECTIVE

to give peace a chance,

and stop and smell the _____, or do a little dance.
                          PLURAL NOUN

Love your neighbors, love your friends, love your _____, too—
                                                    NOUN

and love the good ol' USA—the red, the _____, and the blue!
                                          COLOR

Extend your _____ in friendship to everyone you meet.
              PART OF THE BODY

Invite a stranger to _____, or bring a stray
                         VERB

_____ home to eat.
    NOUN

These random acts of _____ will put a smile on a face,
                         PLURAL NOUN

and they'll _____ transform (the) _____
               ADVERB   A PLACE

into a better place!

MAD LIBS® is fun to play with friends, but you can also play it by yourself! To begin with, DO NOT look at the story on the page below. Fill in the blanks on this page with the words called for. Then, using the words you have selected, fill in the blank spaces in the story.

Now you've created your own hilarious MAD LIBS® game!

TIE-DYE FOR FASHION

ADJECTIVE _____

ADJECTIVE _____

NOUN _____

ADJECTIVE _____

NOUN _____

PLURAL NOUN _____

PLURAL NOUN _____

PART OF THE BODY (PLURAL) _____

NOUN _____

ADJECTIVE _____

NUMBER _____

TYPE OF LIQUID _____

NOUN _____

ADJECTIVE _____

PART OF THE BODY (PLURAL) _____

MAD LIBS

TIE-DYE FOR FASHION

Tie-dyeing is a/an _____ way to dye your clothing so you
ADJECTIVE

can look like a/an _____ hippie. Here are some instructions
ADJECTIVE

for tie-dyeing your own _____ :
NOUN

1. Select a/an _____ article of clothing and use
    ADJECTIVE

    _____ bands to tie it into different sections.
    NOUN

2. Prepare your dye according to the _____ on the package.
    PLURAL NOUN

3. Remember to put on a pair of rubber _____ over your
    PLURAL NOUN

    _____ to protect them as you dip the
    PART OF THE BODY (PLURAL)

    _____ into the dye.
    NOUN

4. For _____ results, keep the material in the dye for at least
    ADJECTIVE

    _____ minutes. Then remove and rinse under cold
    NUMBER

    running _____ .
    TYPE OF LIQUID

5. Hang on a/an _____ outside to dry.
    NOUN

6. Wear it and enjoy the _____ looks on people's
    ADJECTIVE

    _____ .
    PART OF THE BODY (PLURAL)

MAD LIBS® is fun to play with friends, but you can also play it by yourself! To begin with, DO NOT look at the story on the page below. Fill in the blanks on this page with the words called for. Then, using the words you have selected, fill in the blank spaces in the story.

Now you've created your own hilarious MAD LIBS® game!

YOUR GOOD FORTUNE

PERSON IN ROOM _____

NOUN _____

VERB _____

PART OF THE BODY _____

NOUN _____

PLURAL NOUN _____

PERSON IN ROOM _____

CELEBRITY _____

NOUN _____

A PLACE _____

ADJECTIVE _____

ADVERB _____

PLURAL NOUN _____

VERB ENDING IN "ING" _____

ADJECTIVE _____

ADJECTIVE _____

ADJECTIVE _____

PART OF THE BODY (PLURAL) _____

NOUN _____

MAD LIBS®

YOUR GOOD FORTUNE

When I entered the room, Madame _____, the
PERSON IN ROOM

famous _____-teller, gestured for me to _____.
NOUN VERB

"What do you wish to know?" she asked as she prepared to read my

_____. "Will I marry a handsome _____?"
PART OF THE BODY NOUN

I asked. She replied, "Yes. Two _____ named
PLURAL NOUN

_____ and _____ think you are the
PERSON IN ROOM CELEBRITY

prettiest, smartest _____ in all of (the) _____.
NOUN A PLACE

Only one will make you truly _____, so you must choose
ADJECTIVE

_____." "Will I be successful?" I asked. "You will find fame
ADVERB

and _____ with your _____ skills," she
PLURAL NOUN VERB ENDING IN "ING"

responded. "But will I be happy?" "Yes, you will always be surrounded

by a/an _____ family and _____ friends who
ADJECTIVE ADJECTIVE

will put you on a/an _____ pedestal and worship at your
ADJECTIVE

_____." *Wow*, I thought. *All that and she hasn't used*
PART OF THE BODY (PLURAL)

her crystal _____ *yet!*
NOUN

MAD LIBS® is fun to play with friends, but you can also play it by yourself! To begin with, DO NOT look at the story on the page below. Fill in the blanks on this page with the words called for. Then, using the words you have selected, fill in the blank spaces in the story.

Now you've created your own hilarious MAD LIBS® game!

HALL MONITOR

PERSON IN ROOM _____

NOUN _____

ADJECTIVE _____

NOUN _____

VERB ENDING IN "ING" _____

ADJECTIVE _____

ADJECTIVE _____

NOUN _____

NOUN _____

ADJECTIVE _____

ARTICLE OF CLOTHING _____

VERB ENDING IN "ING" _____

NOUN _____

TYPE OF FOOD _____

PLURAL NOUN _____

VERB _____

NOUN _____

MAD LIBS

HALL MONITOR

My name is _____. I'm the _____ monitor
           PERSON IN ROOM   NOUN

and peacekeeper here at _____ _____ Memorial
                            ADJECTIVE   NOUN

School. It's my duty to keep the students _____
                                           VERB ENDING IN "ING"

through the halls in a/an _____ and orderly fashion.
                              ADJECTIVE

Originally, I wasn't sure I was _____ enough for this job.
                                    ADJECTIVE

I'm not the strongest _____ in school, and I don't claim to
                           NOUN

be the smartest _____, either. But I have the _____ ability
                     NOUN   ADJECTIVE

to sense when someone has something up their _____.
                                              ARTICLE OF CLOTHING

So heed this warning: If you're thinking about _____
                                               VERB ENDING IN "ING"

in the hallways without a/an _____ pass or planning to
                                  NOUN

start an all-out _____ fight in the cafeteria, forget about it.
                   TYPE OF FOOD

I have _____ in the back of my head. You can run, but you
          PLURAL NOUN

can't _____, and you'll be in the principal's _____
           VERB   NOUN

in no time flat.

MAD LIBS® is fun to play with friends, but you can also play it by yourself! To begin with, DO NOT look at the story on the page below. Fill in the blanks on this page with the words called for. Then, using the words you have selected, fill in the blank spaces in the story.

Now you've created your own hilarious MAD LIBS® game!

FAMOUS HIPPIES IN HISTORY

ADJECTIVE _____

A PLACE _____

VERB _____

PLURAL NOUN _____

PERSON IN ROOM _____

ADJECTIVE _____

PLURAL NOUN _____

ADJECTIVE _____

PLURAL NOUN _____

PERSON IN ROOM _____

PLURAL NOUN _____

ADJECTIVE _____

ADJECTIVE _____

PLURAL NOUN _____

NOUN _____

PERSON IN ROOM _____

NOUN _____

PLURAL NOUN _____

ADJECTIVE _____

NOUN _____

MAD☺LIBS®

FAMOUS HIPPIES IN HISTORY

The hippie lifestyle may be a thing of the past, but many _____
<u>ADJECTIVE</u>

hippies made (the) _____ a better place in which to live,
<u>A PLACE</u>

work, and _____. Here's a look at a few of those
<u>VERB</u>

_____ of the 1960s:
<u>PLURAL NOUN</u>

- **Barefoot** _____ was a/an _____
  <u>PERSON IN ROOM</u>   <u>ADJECTIVE</u>

  songwriter who wrote about love and _____. His
  <u>PLURAL NOUN</u>

  _____ music inspired millions of _____
  <u>ADJECTIVE</u>   <u>PLURAL NOUN</u>

  everywhere.

- **Crazy Daisy** _____ was known for weaving
  <u>PERSON IN ROOM</u>

  beautiful _____ into her hair. This _____
  <u>PLURAL NOUN</u>   <u>ADJECTIVE</u>

  flower child also painted many _____ murals depicting
  <u>ADJECTIVE</u>

  _____ living in peace and _____.
  <u>PLURAL NOUN</u>   <u>NOUN</u>

- **Grandma Groovy Pants** _____ was an anti-
  <u>PERSON IN ROOM</u>

  _____ activist who championed equality for all
  <u>NOUN</u>

  _____ in our society and supported her _____
  <u>PLURAL NOUN</u>   <u>ADJECTIVE</u>

  beliefs by marching for justice and _____.
  <u>NOUN</u>

MAD LIBS® is fun to play with friends, but you can also play it by yourself! To begin with, DO NOT look at the story on the page below. Fill in the blanks on this page with the words called for. Then, using the words you have selected, fill in the blank spaces in the story.

Now you've created your own hilarious MAD LIBS® game!

THE SUMMER OF LOVE LETTERS, PART 1

PLURAL NOUN _____

ADJECTIVE _____

PLURAL NOUN _____

ADJECTIVE _____

ADJECTIVE _____

ADVERB _____

PLURAL NOUN _____

ADJECTIVE _____

PART OF THE BODY _____

ADVERB _____

A PLACE _____

ADJECTIVE _____

NOUN _____

PLURAL NOUN _____

ADJECTIVE _____

ADJECTIVE _____

PERSON IN ROOM _____

MAD☺LIBS®
THE SUMMER OF LOVE
LETTERS, PART 1

I was in the attic going through some old _____ when,

PLURAL NOUN

to my _____ surprise, I came across my parents' old love

ADJECTIVE

_____. Here's one of Mom's most _____

PLURAL NOUN   ADJECTIVE

letters:

My _____ Hippie Honey,

ADJECTIVE

I miss you _____—more than _____

ADVERB   PLURAL NOUN

can say! I miss your _____ smile. I miss the way my

ADJECTIVE

_____ beats when your eyes stare _____ into

PART OF THE BODY   ADVERB

mine. I miss going for long walks at (the) _____ at

A PLACE

sunset. Do you ever picture us spending the rest of our _____

ADJECTIVE

lives together? I do. I dream of our living in a cozy house with a picket

_____. I know in my heart of _____

NOUN   PLURAL NOUN

that I want to grow _____ with you.

ADJECTIVE

With all my _____ love,

ADJECTIVE

_____

PERSON IN ROOM

MAD LIBS® is fun to play with friends, but you can also play it by yourself! To begin with, DO NOT look at the story on the page below. Fill in the blanks on this page with the words called for. Then, using the words you have selected, fill in the blank spaces in the story.

Now you've created your own hilarious MAD LIBS® game!

THE SUMMER OF LOVE LETTERS, PART 2

ADJECTIVE _____

ADJECTIVE _____

PLURAL NOUN _____

NOUN _____

PLURAL NOUN _____

ADJECTIVE _____

PART OF THE BODY _____

PART OF THE BODY _____

NOUN _____

PART OF THE BODY _____

NOUN _____

PART OF THE BODY _____

NOUN _____

SILLY WORD _____

NOUN _____

ADVERB _____

NOUN _____

PERSON IN ROOM _____

MAD LIBS®
THE SUMMER OF LOVE
LETTERS, PART 2

Now, here's a/an _____ letter from my _____
                        ADJECTIVE   ADJECTIVE

dad to my mom:

To the girl of my _____,
                    PLURAL NOUN

Not a/an _____ goes by that I don't think of you.
                NOUN

I don't know what I did to deserve you, but I thank my lucky

_____ that I am so _____ to be the one who
    PLURAL NOUN   ADJECTIVE

holds the key to your _____. I dreamed last night that I
                        PART OF THE BODY

asked your father for your _____ in marriage. With a/an
                            PART OF THE BODY

_____ on his face, he nodded his _____ and
        NOUN   PART OF THE BODY

said, "Yes." When I awakened, I realized I don't want to wait until I

graduate from _____ school. I want to come home now,
                    NOUN

drop down on one _____, put a diamond _____
                    PART OF THE BODY   NOUN

on your finger, and pop the question. When you say, "_____,"
                                                        SILLY WORD

you'll make me the happiest _____ in the world.
                                NOUN

Truly, madly, _____ in love with you,
                    ADVERB

Your _____-to-be, _____
        NOUN   PERSON IN ROOM

MAD LIBS® is fun to play with friends, but you can also play it by yourself! To begin with, DO NOT look at the story on the page below. Fill in the blanks on this page with the words called for. Then, using the words you have selected, fill in the blank spaces in the story.

Now you've created your own hilarious MAD LIBS® game!

TEAM PEACE

NOUN _____

PLURAL NOUN _____

ADJECTIVE _____

PERSON IN ROOM _____

PLURAL NOUN _____

ADJECTIVE _____

PLURAL NOUN _____

ADJECTIVE _____

VERB _____

ADJECTIVE _____

PLURAL NOUN _____

NOUN _____

ADJECTIVE _____

ADJECTIVE _____

ADJECTIVE _____

PART OF THE BODY _____

NOUN _____

ADJECTIVE _____

MAD LIBS®

TEAM PEACE

It was the day of the most important _____ on the schedule
_____NOUN_____

and the coach knew his team was a bundle of _____. He
_____PLURAL NOUN_____

wisely invited the _____ guru _____ to help
_____ADJECTIVE_____   _____PERSON IN ROOM_____

his players find their inner _____. The guru's pep talk
_____PLURAL NOUN_____

was simple and _____:
_____ADJECTIVE_____

Block out the screaming _____ in the stadium. Focus on
_____PLURAL NOUN_____

becoming one with the _____ ball. The most important
_____ADJECTIVE_____

thing is to believe you can _____ better today than you
_____VERB_____

have in any other _____ game this season. The opposing
_____ADJECTIVE_____

_____ will try to shake your _____, but you
_____PLURAL NOUN_____   _____NOUN_____

must stay calm, cool, and _____, and always be positive. If
_____ADJECTIVE_____

one of your teammates makes a/an _____ play, give him
_____ADJECTIVE_____

a/an _____ pat of encouragement on the _____.
_____ADJECTIVE_____   _____PART OF THE BODY_____

Now put your _____ faces on and go make us
_____NOUN_____

_____!
_____ADJECTIVE_____

MAD LIBS® is fun to play with friends, but you can also play it by yourself! To begin with, DO NOT look at the story on the page below. Fill in the blanks on this page with the words called for. Then, using the words you have selected, fill in the blank spaces in the story.

Now you've created your own hilarious MAD LIBS® game!

GARAGE BAND DEBUT

TYPE OF LIQUID _____

PART OF THE BODY _____

NOUN _____

ADJECTIVE _____

PART OF THE BODY (PLURAL) _____

PLURAL NOUN _____

NOUN _____

ADJECTIVE _____

COLOR _____

PERSON IN ROOM _____

PERSON IN ROOM _____

ADVERB _____

ADJECTIVE _____

NUMBER _____

ADVERB _____

PLURAL NOUN _____

PART OF THE BODY _____

NOUN _____

ADJECTIVE _____

MAD LIBS®

GARAGE BAND DEBUT

As the lights dimmed, I could feel beads of _____ drip down
                                            TYPE OF LIQUID

my _____. The school dance was my band's first real
      PART OF THE BODY

_____ and I was so _____, I was sure everyone
      NOUN   ADJECTIVE

could see my _____ shaking. "Hello,
                PART OF THE BODY (PLURAL)

_____!" I shouted into the micro-_____. "We're
   PLURAL NOUN   NOUN

really happy to be here at your _____ dance. Tonight,
                                    ADJECTIVE

our first song will be '_____ Haze.'" I glanced back at
                            COLOR

_____ on keyboards and _____ on drums
   PERSON IN ROOM   PERSON IN ROOM

(both of whom were sweating _____), took a/an
                                ADVERB

_____ breath, and began the count: "And a one, and a two,
   ADJECTIVE

and a one, two, _____!" The next thing I knew, the audience
                    NUMBER

was cheering _____ and dancing like _____.
                ADVERB   PLURAL NOUN

Even the principal was tapping her _____ on the
                                        PART OF THE BODY

_____. Who knows? A school dance tonight—maybe a/an
   NOUN

_____ record deal tomorrow!
   ADJECTIVE

MAD LIBS® is fun to play with friends, but you can also play it by yourself! To begin with, DO NOT look at the story on the page below. Fill in the blanks on this page with the words called for. Then, using the words you have selected, fill in the blank spaces in the story.

Now you've created your own hilarious MAD LIBS® game!

DID YOU EVER HAVE ONE OF THOSE DAYS?

ADJECTIVE _____

NOUN _____

ADJECTIVE _____

VERB ENDING IN "ING" _____

NUMBER _____

ADJECTIVE _____

NOUN _____

NOUN _____

LETTER OF THE ALPHABET _____

ADJECTIVE _____

ADJECTIVE _____

EXCLAMATION _____

NOUN _____

MAD☺LIBS®
DID YOU EVER HAVE
ONE OF THOSE DAYS?

Dear Diary:

What a/an _____ day! I forgot my gym _____,
           ADJECTIVE   NOUN

so the _____ teacher made me do one hundred
           ADJECTIVE

_____ jacks. I was late getting to homeroom and the
VERB ENDING IN "ING"

teacher had me write _____ times "I promise not to be
                         NUMBER

_____ ever again." As if *that's* not enough, I was in the
    ADJECTIVE

bathroom and dropped my report in the _____! I can't turn
                                        NOUN

in a soaking wet _____, so I'm probably going to get
                  NOUN

a/an _____. Did I mention someone spilled a bowl
      LETTER OF THE ALPHABET

of _____ soup all over me at lunch? And worse than that,
    ADJECTIVE

I bit into an apple and cracked the filling in my _____
                                         ADJECTIVE

molar. _____! I guess I just got up on the wrong side of
      EXCLAMATION

the _____ this morning.
    NOUN

MAD LIBS® is fun to play with friends, but you can also play it by yourself! To begin with, DO NOT look at the story on the page below. Fill in the blanks on this page with the words called for. Then, using the words you have selected, fill in the blank spaces in the story.

Now you've created your own hilarious MAD LIBS® game!

HIPPIE SPEAK, PART 1

ADJECTIVE _____

PLURAL NOUN _____

PERSON IN ROOM _____

NOUN _____

NUMBER _____

ADJECTIVE _____

PERSON IN ROOM _____

ADJECTIVE _____

PART OF THE BODY _____

PLURAL NOUN _____

PLURAL NOUN _____

ADJECTIVE _____

ADJECTIVE _____

VERB (PAST TENSE) _____

A PLACE _____

In addition to their distinctive style of dressing, hippies had their

own _____ language. Here are some of the most popular
ADJECTIVE

_____ :
PLURAL NOUN

- **Groovy** meant cool. *That _____ is one groovy*
  PERSON IN ROOM

  _____ *!*
  NOUN

- **Far-out** was _____ times better than groovy. *My mom's*
  NUMBER

  letting me go to the _____ concert with _____ .
  ADJECTIVE   PERSON IN ROOM

  Far-out!

- To **dig it** was to understand. *When my teacher asked if I understood*

  the _____ homework, I nodded my _____
  ADJECTIVE   PART OF THE BODY

  and said, "I dig it."

- **Threads** referred to clothing. *"Man, between her peace sign*

  _____ *and her tie-dyed _____ , she's got really*
  PLURAL NOUN   PLURAL NOUN

  _____ *threads!"*
  ADJECTIVE

- If something was **a gas**, it meant you had a really _____
  ADJECTIVE

  time. *It was a gas when we _____ with our friends*
  VERB (PAST TENSE)

  at (the) _____ .
  A PLACE

MAD LIBS® is fun to play with friends, but you can also play it by yourself! To begin with, DO NOT look at the story on the page below. Fill in the blanks on this page with the words called for. Then, using the words you have selected, fill in the blank spaces in the story.

Now you've created your own hilarious MAD LIBS® game!

HIPPIE SPEAK, PART 2

NOUN _____

PERSON IN ROOM _____

ADJECTIVE _____

ADJECTIVE _____

NOUN _____

A PLACE _____

NOUN _____

ADJECTIVE _____

ADJECTIVE _____

PERSON IN ROOM _____

ADJECTIVE _____

NOUN _____

ADJECTIVE _____

PLURAL NOUN _____

PART OF THE BODY (PLURAL) _____

NOUN _____

- Your **pad** was your home, or the place where you hung your

  _____ . *Let's go hang out at* _____ *'s pad*
  NOUN   PERSON IN ROOM

  and listen to some _____ *bebop.*
                                ADJECTIVE

- To **crash** meant to sleep. *You look* _____ . *Why don't*
                                                   ADJECTIVE

  you go in the bedroom and crash on the _____ ?
                                                   NOUN

- When you **split**, you left (the) _____ . *As soon as the*
                                            A PLACE

  _____ *rang, we split from school and went shopping for*
  NOUN

  _____ *threads.*
  ADJECTIVE

- **The scene** referred to a place where something _____
                                                       ADJECTIVE

  was going on. If _____ *is in the principal's office,*
                                       PERSON IN ROOM

  it must be a/an _____ *scene.*
                                     ADJECTIVE

- **Happening** described a place where every _____ was
                                                      NOUN

  having fun. Between the _____ *music and the delicious*
                                            ADJECTIVE

  _____ , *that party was happening!*
  PLURAL NOUN

- **Peace out** meant goodbye. *He held up two* _____
                                                      PART OF THE BODY (PLURAL)

  as he left the _____ *and said, "Peace out."*
                                NOUN